They Turned to Stone

by JULIAN MAY

Pictures by JEAN ZALLINGER

SCHOLASTIC BOOK SERVICES

NEW YORK • TORONTO • LONDON • AUCKLAND • SYDNEY

There are many kinds of fossils.

Sometimes a fossil is an animal or a plant
that has been buried and has turned to stone.

Sometimes even a footprint may become a fossil.
The footprint is buried under mud.
Then, after millions of years, the mud turns to stone —
and we have a fossil footprint.

Text copyright © 1965 by Julian May Dikty. Illustrations copyright © 1965 by Jean Zallinger. This edition is published by Scholastic Book Services, a division of Scholastic Magazines, Inc., by arrangement with Holiday House, Inc. The text of this Scholastic edition is the same as the original text except for minor editorial revisions.

7th printing .... September 1971

Printed in the U.S.A.

When you see a stone, pick it up.

Maybe it feels a bit bumpy and strange.

Look at the stone. Look very, very closely.

Maybe it was once alive.

REEF CORAL ANIMAL

FOSSIL FERN

Some stones were alive long, long ago.
Maybe your stone is part of an animal
that once lived in the sea.
Maybe your stone is part of a plant that lived
in a forest millions and millions of years ago.

Maybe your stone was once part of a dinosaur,
or part of a big mammoth
that looked like an elephant.

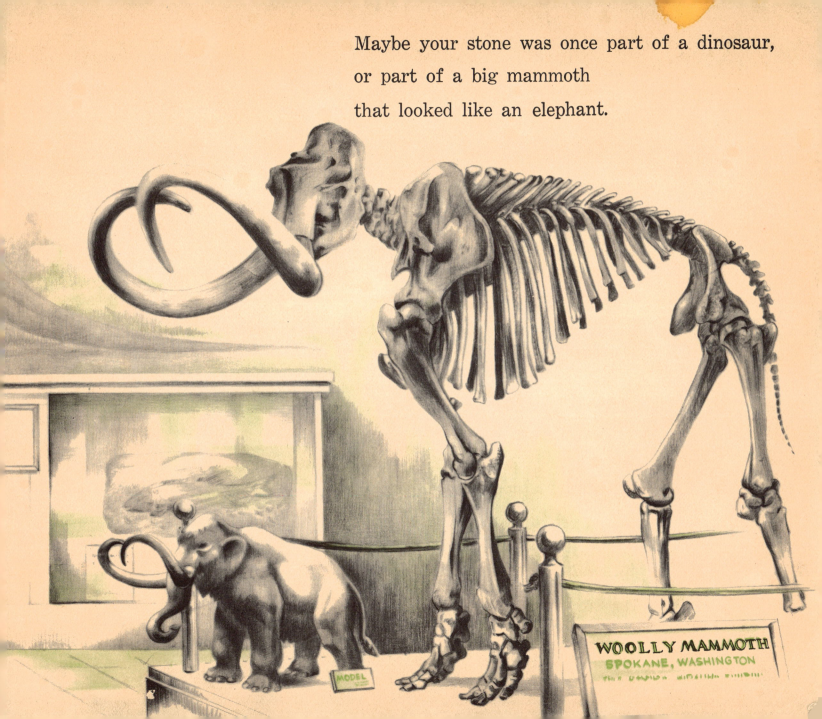

WOOLLY MAMMOTH
SPOKANE, WASHINGTON

MODEL

Sea animals, plants, dinosaurs, mammoths —
they lived long ago and died.

THE SEA 500 MILLION YEARS AGO, WITH A
TRILOBITE 30 INCHES LONG IN FOREGROUND

And some of these plants and animals turned to stone.
Stones of this kind are called fossils.

A FOREST 270 MILLION YEARS AGO

Do most plants and animals turn to stone?

No. It does not happen often.

Most things that die do not turn to stone.

A dead fish on the shore does not
stay there long, so it never becomes a fossil.
The dead fish is food for other animals.
Sea gulls eat some of it.

At night, crabs come and eat some more.

DECAY BACTERIA
AS SEEN UNDER
A MICROSCOPE

Germs feed on the dead fish too.

The germs are called decay bacteria.

We cannot see them because they are so small.

When these bacteria eat something,

we say that the thing decays.

Decay bacteria feed and feed on the fish's flesh.

Soon there is nothing left but a fish skeleton.

Waves and wind and blowing sand

break the skeleton. The bits are scattered

far and wide.

Now the dead fish has disappeared.

Most dead plants and animals disappear in this way.

They do not turn to stone.

But sometimes things are different.

Here is a fish that turned into a fossil.

It was found by a scientist.

It lived long ago in what is now Wyoming.

GREEN RIVER FOSSIL FISH

The fish lived in a lake.

A muddy river flowed nearby.

Mud from the river covered the fish
soon after it died.

Birds and hungry animals could not
find it and eat it.

It lay deep in the mud.

The river poured more and more mud
on the dead fish.
Decay bacteria ate the soft parts.
Only the skeleton was left.
The deep mud helped to save it.

The mud became very, very deep.

After millions of years, the mud turned to stone.

The bony fish skeleton was inside the stone.

All this happened sixty million years ago.

Some day you may go to a place
where there are many fossils.
If you do, look among the rocks.
And if you are very lucky,
you too may find a stone with a fish skeleton
that is sixty million years old.

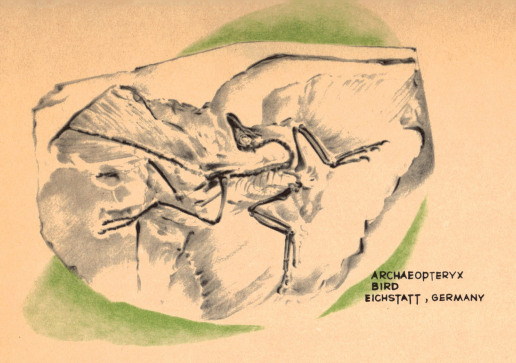

ARCHAEOPTERYX
BIRD
EICHSTATT, GERMANY

PLANT
COLORADO

INSECT
KANSAS

ANNULARIA
HORSETAIL RUSH
BRAIDWOOD, ILLINOIS

Here are pictures of other fossils.
These plants and animals died millions
of years ago. They were all saved
by being buried in mud.
The mud turned to stone,
and the plants and animals became fossils.

How is a fossil formed? Let's see.
Here is a picture of two dinosaurs
that lived seventy-five million years ago
in Canada.
They fought each other and died.

Swamp mud covered the dinosaurs.

Bacteria ate the dinosaurs' flesh.

But they hardly ate the bones at all.

The swamp mud turned to stone.

Water seeped into tiny cracks in the mudstone.

It seeped into the little holes and cracks

in the bones too.

As the water seeped in, it brought very tiny
bits of mineral into the space where
the bones were. Mineral is a hard substance
that makes up stone.

After a long time, all the little cracks and holes in
the bones became filled with this mineral.
The bits of mineral stuck together.

Millions of years passed.
Then one day a fossil hunter found the bones
of the two dinosaurs.
He painted them with shellac.
The shellac kept the bones from breaking.

You can see the dinosaur skeletons today.

They are in a big museum.

Many museums have such fossil skeletons.

Perhaps you can find fossils.

Do you live in the city? Many large buildings

are made of limestone — often called marble.

Fossils are often found in limestone.

Look closely. Sometimes you can see

fossil sea animals in the limestone.

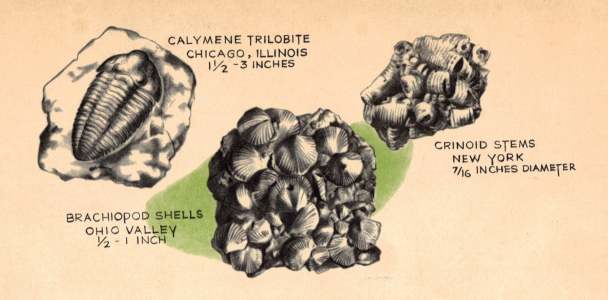

CALYMENE TRILOBITE
CHICAGO, ILLINOIS
1½ - 3 INCHES

CRINOID STEMS
NEW YORK
7/16 INCHES DIAMETER

BRACHIOPOD SHELLS
OHIO VALLEY
½ - 1 INCH

Limestone rocks can often be found in fields
or hills. Crushed rock used in driveways
may be limestone.
Find some limestone that nobody wants.
Crack the pieces with a hammer.
You might find fossils like these.

RECEPTACULITES, FOSSIL SPONGE
UPPER MISSISSIPPI VALLEY
12 - 24 INCHES

CLYPEASTER
SAND DOLLAR, AN ECHINODERM
ISLAND OF MALTA

Look for fossils on the shore.

Here are some strange-looking stones

with fossil sea animals in them.

Try to find slabs of dark, crumbly rock (called shale)
sticking up in a field.
You may be able to find fossil plants in the shale.
Usually all that's left of the plants
is a thin layer of black carbon.

Lumps of coal sometimes have bits of
fossil plants in them too.

WALNUT LEAF
COLORADO

Look for fossils in gullies. And look in places where
a road has been cut through a hill. Once in a while
people find fossil bones sticking out of the hillside.
The fossil is often harder than the crumbly rock
around it. Large fossils should be left
for scientists to remove.

Some fossils break easily.
Sometimes you can save them.
Paint them with shellac
as soon as you uncover them.

See if you can make a fossil collection.
Find the names of any fossils you discover.
Look in books for pictures of them.
Or take your fossils to a museum
and ask someone to help you.

When you pick up a stone, look at it.
Look closely.
Maybe it was once alive.

SOME LIVING THINGS MILLIONS OF YEARS AGO

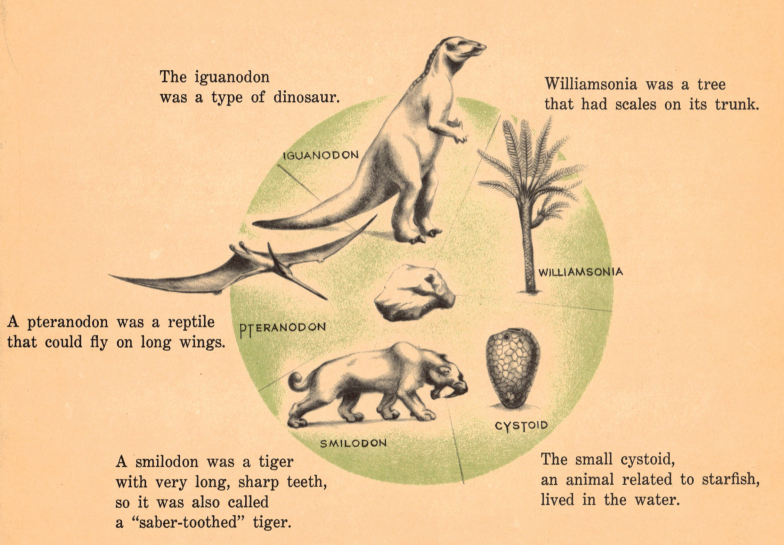

The iguanodon
was a type of dinosaur.

Williamsonia was a tree
that had scales on its trunk.

IGUANODON

WILLIAMSONIA

PTERANODON

A pteranodon was a reptile
that could fly on long wings.

CYSTOID

SMILODON

A smilodon was a tiger
with very long, sharp teeth,
so it was also called
a "saber-toothed" tiger.

The small cystoid,
an animal related to starfish,
lived in the water.

Thanks are due the Chicago Natural History Museum
for the use of reference material for this book.